#NoFear:

A 7-Day Devotional Journal to Overcome Anxiety

C.M. Alvarez

#NoFear: A 7 Day Devotional Journal to Overcome Anxiety

Copyright © 2019 – C.M. Alvarez

Cover Direction: Taylor Alvarez

ISBN-13: 9781711363646

DEDICATION

To my girls: Avery, Taylor, and Peyton

A Gift for You

Thank you for purchasing #NoFear: A 7-Day Devotional. As a thank you, I invite you to download a free guide, "5 Steps: How to Read the Bible to Hear God"

http://raisedtowalk.org/no-more-fear

CONTENTS

PREFACE

Before we begin, I want to take a little time to clarify the position from which this devotional is written.

If You Aren't a Christian

If you have never made Jesus the Lord of your life, repenting of your sins and acknowledging Him as Savior, that is the first step.

God is real. Not only is God real, but there are real spiritual forces at work in the world that are in direct opposition to the God who loves you. Because they have no power against the Lord of Lords they will attack you because through you, they can hurt Him because He loves you. They will do everything they can to destroy your joy, your peace of mind, your spiritual well-being, and even your life. (John 10:10)

If you haven't made Jesus the Lord of your life, if you aren't covered by the blood of the Lamb, you are subject to the powers of this world. Fear is a spirit, anxiety is our response. You won't truly be victorious over either unless you are in Christ. Read "The Final Destination" at the end of this book.

If You Are a Christian

When we accept Christ as our Savior, we are justified (made right) in God's sight in that moment. We are born again into a new life and our spirit is made perfect. However, our soul (mind, will, and emotions) and body are still operating in this world. Because of that, the Christian walk is a process of sanctification, cleaning up our body and soul that operates in this fallen world. The writer of Hebrews explains it this way:

> For by one sacrifice he has made perfect forever those who are being made holy. Hebrews 10:14 NIV

Our spirit is "made perfect," it is finished; but we have to walk out the "being made holy." We grow in our knowledge of God. We learn how to walk in His will. The Holy Spirit will not be done perfecting us until we see God face to face.

We must constantly submit ourselves to God. Acknowledging that we, as Christians, have areas in our lives where we need to mature, be purified, or bring into alignment with God's will is not a sign that we are not "spiritual." It is a sign that we are continuing to listen to the prompting of the Holy Spirit. We never stop needing a Savior, so be quick to confess any areas the Holy Spirit brings to your mind. Read 2 Peter 1 which expounds on this.

> For this very reason, make every effort to add to your faith goodness; and to goodness, knowledge; and to knowledge, self-control; and to self-control, perseverance; and to perseverance, godliness; and to godliness, mutual affection; and to mutual affection, love. For if you possess these qualities in increasing measure, they will keep you from being ineffective and unproductive in your knowledge of our Lord Jesus Christ. But whoever does not have them is nearsighted and blind, forgetting that they have been cleansed from their past sins.

> Therefore, my brothers and sisters, make every effort to confirm your calling and election. For if you do these things, you will never stumble, and you will receive a rich welcome into the eternal kingdom of our Lord and Savior Jesus Christ. 2 Peter 1:5-10 NIV)

INTRODUCTION

There were giants in the land.[1] The footsore group trekking across the wilderness had, as their ancestor Abraham before them, left the land that they knew for a promise. A promise of their own land where they could be their own people free from oppression.

Miraculous events had turned their former masters into their sponsors. They were showered with gifts and wealth as they left. They had everything they needed to start anew. When it seemed that they would be taken back once again into captivity, once again they were miraculously delivered . . . their oppressors to be seen no more.

Their path was clear before them. They followed the presence of Yahweh, a cloud by day and a pillar of fire by night, and now they had arrived at their destination . . . a land which had been promised to them generations ago . . . but there were giants.

In spite of all the provisions and all the seemingly impossible situations God had already brought them through, for some reason, this seemed different. The giants seemed too big for the God who had already defeated those of Egypt. They did not feel equipped or prepared for what waited for them in the land, even the abundance and prosperity that they saw waiting for them was not enough to take a risk.

The excitement and anticipation they had felt since the Red Sea crossing when their Egyptian oppressors were taken out by the same water which had given them safe passage began to fade. Although two of the spies, Jacob and Caleb, were still enthusiastic and encouraged the rest to trust God and prepare for battle, the other ten spies spread a bad report, discontent, and discouragement. Those negative words gained more traction than the words of faith.

---

[1] The account of the 12 spies entering Canaan is found in Numbers 13

They were afraid, and because of this fear, an entire generation lost their promised blessing.

Overcoming Fear

If you're like me, you've read the account of the Exodus multiple times and wondered, "What were they thinking?" How could they experience the things during their deliverance from Egypt and lose heart less than two weeks later? But are we any different? If you have been a Christian for any length of time, how many times have you seen God work in your life and yet how often do we allow the circumstances of life to overwhelm us and strike fear into our hearts?

Too often, fear is the enemy that steals our joy, obscures our blessings, and blockades the destiny God has for each of us. Like the Israelites coming out of Egypt, we forget what God has done for us in the past, we are blinded to what He is currently doing in our lives . . . when obstacles seem too big, we let what we see override what God has said.

> Don't be afraid, for I am with you.
>
> Don't be discouraged, for I am your God.
>
> I will strengthen you and help you.
>
> I will hold you up with my victorious right hand. Isaiah 41:10 NLT

This is the truth of which we need to remind ourselves, God has a plan for each one of us. He has a plan for me, and He has a specific plan for you. However, for each one of us, there will come a time when we have to put our trust in God, to have faith in spite of the circumstances in front of us which seem overwhelming. We all face giants at one time or another.

When we begin on the path, often the faith of others can carry us for a while. This was so with the Israelites. They just stood and watched as Moses and Aaron faced down Pharaoh and his sorcerers. There was no cost, nothing they had to commit to. After the third plague, they just watched as God preserved and protected them from the tribulation that embroiled the rest of the nation.

Finally, after the ninth plague, they were told, "You have to choose. Do you put your faith in the Salvation of the God of Abraham or will you stay as you are here?'

Just as God placed His hand of protection on the Israelites who put their trust in Him, evidenced by placing the blood of a lamb on the doorpost, so God has said He will rescue all those who call on Him.

"Because he has set his love upon Me, therefore I will deliver him;

I will set him on high, because he has known My name." - Psalm 91:14

We have a God who has good plans for us.

For I know the plans I have for you," says the Lord. "They are plans for good and not for disaster, to give you a future and a hope. Jeremiah 29:11 NLT[2]

---

[2] I occasionally come across a commentator that dismisses this verse as one for Christians to claim today. They will say things like it was only for the Jews, and claiming that verse as a promise for all who believe in Him is taking the passage out of context.

It is true that we always have to keep in mind the original circumstances which the book was written to and how the original audience would have understood it. However, the God described and acting in the Old Testament is the same God we have faith in today. If He was faithful then, He will be faithful now.

This is the context. After decades of warnings from prophets of God to repent, judgment for the Jewish nation came. They were taken into captivity in Babylon. Some of their religious leaders and false prophets were promising a quick return. Jeremiah told them it was not to be so. That they would be in captivity for 70 years.

The reason for this judgment was that they refused to repent and acknowledge their sins. This is the more of the passage.

"10 This is what the Lord says: "You will be in Babylon for seventy years. But then I will come and do for you all the good things I have promised, and I will bring you home again. 11 For I know the plans I have for you," says the Lord. "They are plans for good and not for disaster, to give you a future and a hope. 12 In those days when you pray, I will listen. 13 If you look for me wholeheartedly, you will find me. 14 I will be found by you," says the Lord. "I will end your captivity and restore your fortunes. I will gather you out of the nations where I sent you and will bring you home again to your own land." Jeremiah 29:10-11

We have a God who will complete the work he has begun in our lives.

> The Lord will accomplish what concerns me;
>
> Your lovingkindness, O Lord, is everlasting;
>
> Do not forsake the works of Your hands. Psalm 138:8 NASB
>
> And let us run with endurance the race God has set before us. We do this by keeping our eyes on Jesus, the champion who initiates and perfects our faith. Hebrews 12:1b-2 NLT

Just like the Israelites, we will encounter some giants. Circumstances that seem to make God a liar. The corruption will seem too great, the addiction too strong, or the diagnosis too dire. When the giant you are facing seems too big for God to handle, remember this . . . Jesus was dead. He had been in the grave for three days. When it seemed like it was all over, God proved His power and won the ultimate victory.

When you make Jesus the Lord of your life, the same Holy Spirit that raised Christ

---

As you can see, even during the time of judgment, God had a promise for the people. He was waiting to be found by them when they turned their hearts wholly to Him.

The condition for restoration was repentance.

If you have read the account of Israel's return, you know that not only did they return, but they returned financed by their former oppressors. The cost for the travel and restoration of Jerusalem and the temple was financed by Cyrus the Persian king. Later, during the time of Artaxerxes, what was meant as a literal death knell for the entire Jewish people ended up prospering and annihilating their enemies.

These "good plans" Jeremiah referred to are the same that Paul references in Romans 8:28.

"And we know that in all things God works for the good of those who love him, who have been called according to his purpose." (NIV)

God and His Salvation are the same yesterday, today, and forever (Hebrews 13:8) He works out the good for those who love Him.

from the grave[3] is within you.[4]

As C.S. Lewis writes in *Surprised by Joy*, the quickest way to overcome an emotion is to "start examining the passion itself.[5]" This is the premise of this devotional and journal. We are going to take a look at those "giants," the things in our life that seem bigger than God's power and His grace. As big of a role those things play in our lives, they often go unnoticed. They are truly, the "elephant in the room."

---

[3] Note: if you are a Christian and have an intellectual assent to the truth of the resurrection but are without an assurance of the truth and historicity of Jesus' actual resurrection, I encourage you to read scholarship in this area. As C.S. Lewis wrote in his autobiography Surprised by Joy, having to acknowledge that the resurrection was historical fact knocked the foundation out of his stance as an atheist. How much more should those evidences encourage us as Christians and strengthen our faith.

Lee Strobel's *A Case for Christ* is a very accessible and engaging explanation of the facts. *The Case for the Resurrection of Jesus* by Gary Habermas and Mike Licona lays out the four minimal facts that prove the resurrection. I have gone through these four facts with my third grade Sunday school class.

If you are interested in an exhaustive resource, *The Resurrection of Jesus: A New Historiographical Approach,* also by Mike Licona, is a good resource.

[4] Romans 8:11 NLT "The Spirit of God, who raised Jesus from the dead, lives in you. And just as God raised Christ Jesus from the dead, he will give life to your mortal bodies by this same Spirit living within you."

[5] C.S. Lewis, *Surprised by Joy*, in *The Beloved Works of C.S. Lewis*, The Family Christian Library. (Grand Rapids, MI: Family Christian Press, 1998), 120.

Lewis reflects on the difference between "contemplation" and "enjoyment." To put it most simply, just as you cannot play baseball while analyzing baseball, you cannot experience or be in the midst of an emotion while examining it.

In my testimony at the end of the journal, I talk about the difference between "knowing" and doing or being. It is the same concept. A few excerpts from *Surprised by Joy*.

" It seemed to me self-evident that one essential property of love, hate, fear, hope or desire was attention to their object . . . You cannot hope and also think about hoping at the same moment; for in hope we look to hope's object and we interrupt this by (so to speak) turning round to look at the hope itself . . . The surest means of disarming an anger or lust was to turn your attention from the girl or the insult and start examining the passion itself."

Working Through This Journal

For each day, there is a reflection, verses to meditate on, and a song that goes along with the theme of the day. Before you begin, I encourage you to pause and ask the Holy Spirit to speak to you in the passages and to reveal any areas in your life that it is time to cleanse, heal, restore, or renew. As you answer the questions for the day's reflection, listen for the Holy Spirit speaking to your heart.

I have chosen a song to begin our journey, "The God who Sees" by Lauren Mullen. (On Youtube: https://www.youtube.com/watch?v=l6sX4Vw8mx0)

For a full playlist of songs to accompany this devotional, as well as printable Scripture cards to use as you study the word, visit my site http://raisedtowalk.org/no-fear

.

GETTING STARTED

When we are working on our health and fitness, we track our progress. We journal what we eat, how many steps we took, and how we exercise. Our spiritual journey should be the same way.

There was a period in my life when I was under extreme and extended stress. Operating in anxiety was such a part of my life that I didn't even recognize the stress. I remember laying in bed at night with my teeth gritted. I had no physical pain, just stress. Two years after the situation causing the stress ended, I was sitting at an event with my girls and I realized . . . I was at peace. I was relaxed. I wasn't worried or anxious or on edge. I had been anxious so long that I didn't even remember what it felt like to be otherwise.

When you are in the middle of a mess, and you've been there for a while, sometimes you don't know what normal looks like anymore. That is something else to ask God for, that He help you recognize where you should be so that you know when you are not. If this is the place where you are right now, look for those moments of peace. Once you have that moment, remember it. That is the goal.

In order to see the impact of what God has done for us and how far you have come, it is helpful to keep track of where you begin and where you end.

If you already journal, this is an easy task. If not and it seems like an overwhelming process, simply track how your day went on a calendar. It doesn't have to be complicated.

To begin, just track a few things:

Emotional State: Just like hospitals have a pain scale, use a scale to rank your emotional state for the day. A zero means you are at perfect peace. A ten is a high state of anxiety where you can't function, you can't sleep, you can't think, and you can't rest.

Activity: What did you do that day. Just write a few words as a reminder.

People: Who were you around? Are there certain people who trigger anxiety for you? If so, is there an area where you need to forgive them personally or is it that they remind you in some way of a person in your past towards whom you hold hard feelings?

Diet: What did you eat today? If certain foods begin to stand out as related to high anxiety days, keep a more detailed food journal. We are tri-part beings: mind, body, and spirit. Being out of whack in one area affects the other two . . . and this includes food.

Quiet Time: Our peace comes from the Prince of Peace. Are you spending time daily in prayer and reading his word?

Track these things for a month and then go back and review. What stands out to you?

7 DAY DEVOTIONAL

#NoFear

DAY 1: FEAR, A BASIC EMOTION

With three kids, most of the movies I watch are cartoons or animations. I am well versed in the Pixar and Disney film catalog. One of my favorite films from 2015 was *Inside Out*, an animated film that is told from the perspective of the heroine's emotions.

In the opening scene when the baby girl opens her eyes and sees her parents' smile, the first emotion that arrives in the landscape of her mind is Joy, and it is Joy that plays the dominant role in her mind and personality until the crisis in the movie. Joy's fellow roommates in the mind of the heroine, Anger, Fear, Disgust, and Sadness, quickly arrived

As I was watching, I was excited for a moment. I thought, "are they going to talk about spiritual realities?" The answer to that is no. The movie was based on psychological research which states that there are seven emotions common to all people across cultures: joy, anger, fear, disgust, contempt, sadness, and surprise. The film writers narrowed it down to five for narrative purposes.

These feelings of fear, anger, sadness, disgust, and contempt are part of our natural fallen state; however, this is not what God originally intended nor are those feelings part of His plan for those who are walking with Him. 2 Timothy 1:7 clearly states, "For God has not given us a **spirit of fear** but of power, and of love, and of a sound mind."

Furthermore, rather than disgust, contempt, and anger, the Holy Spirit empowers us in Christ to produce different fruit: love, joy, peace, patience, kindness, goodness, faithfulness, gentleness, and self-control. (Galatians 5:22-23).

Fear is something that we all deal with, even though we may not acknowledge it. Instead of saying, "I'm afraid," we say that we are feeling anxious, stressed, or depressed. Fear is a spirit, one which is not of God, and we are to stand against it.

Song of the Day

"The Breakup Song" by Francesca Battistelli

On Youtube: https://www.youtube.com/watch?v=H0wpP5o7xpI

Reflection

What are my greatest fears?

_____

_____

_____

_____

_____

_____

_____

_____

How do I feel when fear comes upon me and anxious thoughts creep up?

_____

_____

_____

_____

_____

_____

Verses for the Day

2 Timothy 1:7 "For God has not given us a spirit of fear, but of power and of love and of a sound mind." KJV

Psalm 56:3 "When I am afraid, I will put my trust in you." NASB

1 John 4:4 "You are from God, little children, and have overcome them. For greater is he that is in you than he that is in the world." NASB

Prayer

In a quiet time with God, thank Him for His great love and care for you. Confess the areas where you have fear and issues where you struggle handing them over to Him. Ask him to build your faith particularly in those areas and to give you grace to trust in Him.

Day 2: Fear of Discovery

Looking through the verses on fear, anxiety, and worry, I found that the first fear was that of discovery. When Adam and Eve sinned by ignoring the one restriction God placed on them, not only were they then aware of the wide range of possibilities of wrong choices, but they experienced something they had not before . . . Fear.

Imagine what that must have been like, to have walked in the presence of God and to be in constant communion with Him, and then to have that closeness shut off, the door to intimacy closed. Not only that, but there was this new thing, their bodies were responding differently, their brains were flooded with strange and dark thoughts, confusion reigned.

It was in the midst of this confusion that God came for His time of fellowship and instead of joyously meeting Him face to face, they hid. (Genesis 3:4) When God searched and called them out, Adam said: "I heard the sound of You in the garden, and I was afraid because I was naked, so I hid myself." (Genesis 3:10)

Was Adam telling God something that He didn't know? Of course not. God knew not only exactly when and how Adam sinned but foresaw that he would and established His plan before the creation of the world taking it into account. (Ephesians 1:4-5) There is nothing so dark, so secret, and so hidden that God doesn't already know about it.

Not only does God know exactly how you are, but He knows you better than you know yourself because He is the one who knows who He created you to be, "holy and without fault in his eyes." (Ephesians 1:4)

Even before He made the world He had you in mind. He knew exactly when you would be born, the friends you would have, the things you would love, every frustration, every crisis, and every triumph. Every hair on your head is numbered

(Luke 12:7) and no tear has gone unnoticed, He has caught every one. (Psalm 56:8)

God loves you.

He not only wants to have a relationship with you but a close one. If there is a thing in your life that is blocking your relationship with Him, talk to Him about it. Don't feel like you have to fix it yourself or get it right first. That is what Jesus died for. He died to make us right with God. It is impossible to do it on our own.

Song of the Day

"I'm Listening" by Chris McClarney

On Youtube: https://www.youtube.com/watch?v=nT8iKdwbKdU

Reflection

What is the closest you have felt to God?

_____

_____

_____

_____

_____

What was significant about that time in your life?

_____

_____

_____

_____

_____

Do you feel close to God now? If not, what do you feel is the reason?

_____

_____

_____

_____

Verses for the Day

"If we confess our sins, he is faithful and just to forgive us our sins and to cleanse us from all unrighteousness." 1 John 1:9 KJV

"But God showed his great love for us by sending Christ to die for us while we were still sinners. And since we have been made right in God's sight by the blood of Christ, he will certainly save us from God's condemnation. For since our friendship with God was restored by the death of his Son while we were still his enemies, we will certainly be saved through the life of his Son. So now we can rejoice in our wonderful new relationship with God because our Lord Jesus Christ has made us friends of God." Romans 3:9-11 NLT

Prayer

Father,

Thank you that you sent your son Jesus to die on the cross so that we can be in relationship and communion with you. I submit myself to you, please show me anything in my life that is not pleasing to you. Thank you that you have already provided atonement for me in the blood of Jesus. I confess and submit it to you, covering it with the precious blood of Jesus. Wipe me clean of sin and make me innocent of guilt.

In Jesus's name, Amen.

DAY 3: FEAR OF INSECURITY

When researching fear, I was somewhat surprised to find that the number one fear reported by Americans is the fear of government corruption. Fifty-eight percent said that they were "afraid or very afraid." There were a number of other fears listed that fell into this same grouping: government tracking of data (41%); gun control (36.5%); Obamacare (35%); illegal immigration (29%); and drones (20%).[6] Does this surprise you? I'll have to admit, it did surprise me a little.

What we fear losing is evidence of where we put our trust.

We are extremely fortunate in the United States. We have had a relatively stable civil government since our country's inception with the notable exception of the Civil War. Our government has a solid foundation and, for the most part, our citizenship is one that respects and honors that stability. We don't have kangaroo courts or sham elections. We can go and vote without having to fear that we will be shot at the polls.

We aren't Afghanistan and we aren't Iraq. Yet government corruption is the number one reported fear in America.

Why is this? Is it because our government is where we have placed our trust? Have we put our reliance for our safety in man?

Here's the reality, our government *is* corrupt in that there is corruption within. It is corrupt because it is made up of fallen humans, individuals with weaknesses and prejudices. People who, just like the rest of us, often make decisions reacting out of fear rather than analyzing the best or right course of action.

We are blessed in the U.S. in that our government was formed with that fallen

---

[6] The Chapman University Survey of American Fears. Chapman University. 2015.
https://blogs.chapman.edu/wilkinson/2015/10/13/americas-top-fears-2015/

nature in mind. We have checks and balances so that each person in each branch is held accountable. However, you can't put your trust in the government. You can't put your trust in the Republican or Democratic party. You can't put your trust in whether you can own a gun or who is allowed in or who is kept out.

None of these things can ensure your security.

It is God alone that is our sure security. Faith in anything else is a false hope.

Do you believe that? If anxiety begins to rise, reflect on these verses:

Song of the Day

Come Alive by Lauren Daigle

https://www.youtube.com/watch?v=7XAeyFagceQ

Reflection

Have worries about the government or your security kept you up at night?

_____

_____

_____

_____

_____

Have you placed more confidence in who holds a public office than in God and His ability to direct affairs?

_____

_____

_____

_____

_____

Verses for the Day

God's 911

> Those who live in the shelter of the Most High will find rest in the shadow of the Almighty.
>
> This I declare about the Lord: He alone is my refuge, my place of safety;
>
> > he is my God, and I trust him.
>
> For he will rescue you from every trap and protect you from deadly disease.
>
> He will cover you with his feathers.
>
> > He will shelter you with his wings.
>
> > His faithful promises are your armor and protection.
>
> Psalm 91:1-4 NLT

For he will hide me in his shelter in the day of trouble; he will conceal me under the cover of his tent; he will lift me high upon a rock. Psalm 27:5 ESV

"Even if everyone else is a liar, God is true." Romans 3:4 NLT

Prayer

Thank you, Father, that you are our strength and our shield. I thank you that you will never leave me or forsake me. I thank you for the blessing of the country where you have placed me and that you have preserved this nation since its founding. Above all, I put my trust in you. You alone are the rock of my faith. When I become anxious or worried, please forgive me and build my faith through your Holy Spirit. Thank you for your unfailing love and mercy.

In Jesus's name Amen.

Day 4: Fear of Rejection

Social anxiety, fear of public speaking, agoraphobia, these are all ways that the fear of rejection manifests. We are afraid of what people will think of us and if they will accept us.

We fear not being accepted. When we are accepted, we fear jeopardizing that relationship or position. If a relationship or connection ends, it can rock our sense of identity.

It hurts when close attachments end. It hurts when we are betrayed. It hurts when the relationships we thought we had don't turn out to be anything like we thought them to be.

When we look to others for validation of our worth, we will always be under the power of this particular fear. Any time you make your sense of identity about another person, you are setting that person up to disappoint you. No one else, not even a spouse, can complete the person God means for you to be. They can support and enhance the vision God has for the person that is you, just as you can for them, but only God can fulfill it.

Sometimes that fear of rejection leads to isolation. We have been betrayed in the past, and so we think pulling back and cutting ourselves off from those around us will protect us. Isolation is not the plan God has for us or the position He wants us to be in. Just as the essence of God is a relationship of three persons, Father, Son, and Spirit, He designed us as His imagers to be in relationship. We are made to be in relationship with Him and in relationship with others.

So it is natural to seek connections and relationships. The problem comes when we do not first have that core relationship with the One who designed us from which all other healthy relationships flow. Our connection with our Creator must be the relationship we place above all others.

This relationship must be the one that determines the role other people play in our lives. It should not be our friends or coworkers that determine the role God plays in ours.

Jesus knows what it feels like to be rejected. He was mocked by the power players in his society. He was reviled by the public. He was discredited by those he grew up with and even his own family.

> "He was despised and rejected by men, a man of sorrows and acquainted with grief." Isaiah 53:3

However, Jesus was able to bear all of the sorrow and pain because he did not place his trust in men. He placed his trust in God alone. Living as man, it was his relationship with the Heavenly Father that sustained him.

If we want to learn to walk as Jesus did, we must learn to have the same type of relationship with the Father as he had. We must seek Him first, above all and anyone else.

Song of the Day

"He Knows" by Jeremy Camp

On YouTube: https://www.youtube.com/watch?v=OsccUg4TDd8

Reflection

Do you feel anxiety when you are around others or feel like you have to put on a show, to act differently?

_____

_____

_____

_____

_____

Do you feel pressure to behave in a certain way to impress people?

_____

_____

_____

_____

_____

Verses for the Day

Even before he made the world, God loved us and chose us in Christ to be holy and without fault in his eyes. God decided in advance to adopt us into his own family by bringing us to himself through Jesus Christ. This is what he wanted to do and it gave him great pleasure. So we praise God for the glorious grace he has poured out on us who belong to his dear Son. Ephesians 1:4-6 NLT

I pray that from his glorious, unlimited resources he will empower you with inner strength through his Spirit. Then Christ will make his home in your hearts as you trust in him. Your roots will grow down into God's love and keep you strong. And may you have the power to understand, as all God's people should, how wide, how long, how high, and how deep his love is. May you experience the love of Christ, though it is too great to understand fully. Then you will be made complete with all the fullness of life and power that comes from God. How wide how high Ephesians 3:16-19 NLT

Prayer

Thank you, Father, that you love me just as I am. Please forgive me for the times I have put others' opinions over what you have said about me. I reject all of the lies of the enemy, I am the work of your hands and you have made me to be good, blessed, and favored. I plead the blood of Jesus over my mind, thoughts, and attitudes, and ask that the Holy Spirit give me an understanding of just how great your love is for me.

In Jesus's name, Amen.

Day 5: Fear of Not Enough

We don't like to look at it, but fear is very present. It tempts us. It tries to get us to doubt: to doubt God and to doubt ourselves. Fear isn't just something that is in our minds, it affects our whole self . . . mind, body, and spirit. It affects our interactions and relationships with others. It affects the atmosphere around us.

Fear is a brutal dictator if we open the door to it and allow it in. It will take over every area of our lives . . . until we start fighting back. We can't fight what we don't recognize as the enemy. To overcome, we must first identify where fear is operating in our own lives.

This is my story

After my second daughter was born, I had a little bump on my hip. I didn't know what it was, but I dismissed it as something to do with childbirth. A year later, that little bump developed into a boil. I went to the doctor and had it lanced; however, the little bump was still there after it healed.

Then it happened again exactly one year later, that little bump developed into a boil. This time I let it drain on its own and it seemed to heal better than the first time even though there was a tiny knot left deep under the skin.

Eight years passed and while the knot didn't develop into a boil during that time, it would occasionally threaten to flare up. Whenever I went through a period where I ate too much junk food or did not get enough sleep, it would start to swell and hurt. It was as if it were my early detection system, a signal to slow down and take better care of myself.

Then I was asked to help in the planning for an event, one that I believed was significant and could have an impact on influencing opinions. More importantly, it was for a thing that is dear to God's heart.

I was asked because I have experience planning events and I helped because of the people who asked. However, my experience told me that what they wanted to do was impossible in the amount of time we had. We had six weeks to pull together an event similar in scope to the one I had worked on before. For the previous event, if I didn't have plans significantly underway six months ahead of time I had to play catch up.

Six weeks was impossible. I didn't have much hope or high expectations for turnout. My only goal was that we had enough people show up that it wasn't an embarrassment to the cause. I had no target for attendance or goal beyond the prayer, "Please God, don't let this be lame." I saw it as a dry run and a learning experience for the next year.[7]

In that final week going into the event, that bump on my hip began to flare up and develop into a boil. I didn't know what was triggering it. I was eating the way I should and was getting enough sleep. It seemed to come out of the blue. On top of everything else, this could not be happening. I could not be immobilized by a boil in the middle of this event.

So I went to someone for prayer, and not just someone who would pray, but someone who would pray and actually expect God to answer and heal. When I explained the situation and what I thought was triggering it, the person asked me, "What is the stress that you are worrying about right now?"

I thought about it and answered, "Of not enough. Of not having enough, of not doing enough, of not being enough."

How often does the fear of "not enough" hold us back from what God has for us? How often does the lie of "not measuring up" keep us from stepping out and into God's

---

[7] Just in case you are wondering how the event turned out. The event had not been held before in Houston, but it had been held in several other cities nationwide. Afterward, I found out that the average attendance at the event in other locations was 50 people. We had almost 1,000 attend that first year.

It was definitely not "lame."

I saw God bring the pieces together in a way that no one of us involved could have done on our own. We could not have made it happen in the way that it did.

plan for our life, from participating in His plan in the way He has created only us to do?

Here's the reality, none of us are "enough" on our own. Any power we think we have to control outcomes is an illusion. Oh yes, we can plan properly and work diligently, stacking the odds in our favor for success. That diligence on our part is a necessary factor for success.[8]

However, none of us can control outcomes with certainty. Accidents happen, spouses leave, and jobs are lost. Only God can say with certainty a thing will happen.

But here is the awesome thing, when we are in Christ, we are on God's side . . . in His Army. He **is** the winning team. Christ secured the victory at the cross and through Christ, we have, and are, more than enough.

Song of the Day

"God I Look to You" by Bethel Music

On YouTube: https://www.youtube.com/watch?v=LnyXB3Y4P2E

---

[8] Trusting in God is not sitting passively by and waiting for Him to handle our problems as if He were a genie from a bottle. When you read through the Biblical accounts, particularly in the Old Testament, the key was to 1) listen and hear God's voice, and 2) do what he said to do. The person had to step out in faith, believing that God would do what He said He would do. But the project, just like the event I mentioned, was always way bigger than the person could do on their own. God worked through them to bring it about.

Reflection

Do you ever have the feeling that you do not measure up?

_____

_____

_____

_____

_____

Do you ever feel anxiety about what the outcome in a situation will be, that you have to force or manipulate a thing to happen?

_____

_____

_____

_____

_____

Verses for the Day

Luke 1:37 ESV For nothing will be impossible with God.

Matthew 19:26 ESV But Jesus looked at them and said, "With man this is impossible, but with God all things are possible.

Zechariah 4:6b NASB "Not by might nor by power, but by My Spirit," says the Lord of hosts."

Philippians 4:13 NASB I can do all things through him who strengthens me.

Prayer

Father,

We thank you for your faithfulness, that you never leave us or forsake us and that your Word always accomplishes everything it sets out to do. Please forgive me for the times I have tried to go my own way without following your direction and thinking I could do it on my own steam without putting my trust in you. Thank you for your goodness and that you are always more than enough.

In Jesus's name. Amen.

DAY 6: TRUSTING THE OUTCOME

Yesterday, I talked about the fear of "not enough." What insight does this fear shed on our relationship with God?

Beyond believing in Christ for salvation, the Christian walk is identified by several things. We must have faith and believe God, that is our foundation of salvation. "Abraham **believed** God and his **faith** was counted as righteousness." (Genesis 15:6) Even before that day at Calvary, righteousness before God was determined by a person's faith in the salvation of God (Yeshua.)

The other crucial element is **trust**. Sometimes we believe in God and profess faith in Him, but if we really examine our heart . . . our trust is in something else. As we have examined this past week, we can identify what those things are, idols really, by our fear of losing them. When we have trust in anything but God alone, we are at the mercy of fear.

For each of these fears we have talked about, there is an antidote. Peace comes when we really and truly put our trust in the goodness of God and His faithfulness

Fear of Abandonment:

Jeremiah 46:11 "Leave your fatherless children, I will keep them alive, and let your widows trust in me."

Trusting in the Things of this World:

Job 15:31, 34-35 "Let him not trust in emptiness, deceiving himself, for emptiness will be his payment . . . For the company of the godless is barren, and fire consumes the tents of bribery. They conceive trouble and give birth to evil, and their womb prepares deceit."

35

Fear of Security:

Psalm 91:2 "I will say to the Lord, "My refuge and my fortress, my God in whom I trust.

Fear of Financial Loss:

Psalm 49:5-7, 15. "Why should I fear when trouble comes, when enemies surround me? They trust in their wealth and boast of great riches. Yet they cannot redeem themselves from death by paying a ransom to God . . . But as for me, God will redeem my life. He will snatch me from the power of the grave."

Luke 12:21-31 NASB Consider the lilies, how they grow: they neither toil nor spin; but I tell you, not even Solomon in all his glory clothed himself like one of these. But if God so clothes the grass in the field, which is alive today and tomorrow is thrown into the furnace, how much more will he clothe you? You men of little faith! And do not seek what you will eat and what you will drink, and do not keep worrying. For all these things the nations of the world eagerly seek; but your Father knows that you need these things. But seek His kingdom, and these things will be added to you. Do not be afraid, little flock, for your Father has chosen gladly to give you the kingdom.

Fear of Exploitation:

Psalm 62:10-12: Put not trust in extortion, set no vain hopes on robbery; if riches increase, set not your heart on them. Once God has spoken; twice have I heard this: that power belongs to God, and that to you, O Lord, belong steadfast love. For you will render to a man according to his work.

Trusting in God brings peace. Know that he loves you and can be trusted.

Song of the Day

"Rescue" by Lauren Daigle

https://www.youtube.com/watch?v=gYR0xP1j4PY

Reflection

Are there things in your life that you are not trusting God for?

_____

_____

_____

_____

_____

Are there things that you are afraid to turn over to Him?

_____

_____

_____

_____

_____

Verses for the Day

Proverbs 3:5 NIV Trust in the Lord with all your heart, and do not lean on your own understanding.

Psalm 37:5 ESV Commit your way to the Lord, trust in him, and he will act.

Prayer

Father,

Thank you for being patient with me, for understanding my fears even when you have proven yourself over and over again. I know that this fear is not something I can break free of on my own, and I submit this to you. I rebuke this spirit of fear in the name of Jesus and thank you for filling me with the Spirit of Christ and your love. Give me a full understanding of your goodness and faithfulness.

In Jesus's mighty name. Amen.

DAY 7: GOD OUR FATHER

Yesterday, we talked about trust and that trusting in God is the key to ejecting the place fear has in your life. However, that is dependent on our understanding of who God is.

If you think someone is always looking for an opportunity to criticize and condemn you, will you trust them? No. If you think that someone is uninterested in the details of your life, would you confide in them?

I think that is why we often don't go to God for our day-to-day concerns. We don't really believe He's interested and the things don't seem "big" enough to bother Him with. So all the little frustrations and worries add up, one stress piles on top of the other until we become so wired to operating in anxiety that we don't even know what it feels like to be at peace. Peace becomes an unknown quantity that we are at a loss to find on our own.

However, we are not to view God as a distant and detached judge. When the disciples asked Jesus how they should pray, he told them to begin in this way (Matthew 6:9-13):

> Our Father, who is in heaven.

Our Father, someone who loves and cares for us and is intimately concern with our welfare and well-being. We have the right, as His child, to come to Him with all our needs.

> Hallowed be your name.

We don't use the word "hallowed" much anymore. So rarely, in fact, that most would probably associate it with Halloween.[9] However, it means to "honor as holy," to

---

[2] Halloween is actually a condensed form of the original name, All Hallows Eve, which was the

"make holy or consecrate," or acknowledging something as "greatly revered or respected." He is not just Father, but our Great Father.

Your Kingdom Come.

When Jesus walked the earth, he told his disciples, "The Kingdom of God is among you." (Luke 17:21) Jesus Christ, God, come as a human man walking perfectly in God's Will brought God's Kingdom to earth.

Your will be done.

Jesus said, "I only do what I see my Father doing." The miracles he performed were because they were the Father's will. The amazing miracles that he performed were because the Father wanted the blind to see, the deaf to hear, the sick to be well, and the dead to be restored. Jesus trusted, listened, and acted in relationship.

When we accept Christ as our Savior, or as we say in our third grade Sunday school class when we make Jesus the "Boss" of our Life, that same sort of relationship is available to us. The blocks to that are all on our side, we not only have to be willing to trust, but we have to know God for the Good Father that He is.

This knowing, I think, is usually our biggest block. If we understood the fullness and the totality of the goodness of God, if we understood the magnitude of the impact of the atonement . . . what Christ's death really did for us, bringing us out of condemnation . . . we would have no fear at all.

Because that is what Jesus tells us, it is written: "The enemy comes only to steal, kill, and destroy, but I have come that you might have life and have it more abundantly." (John 10:10) Not a depressed, isolated, medicated, bogged down, and restricted life, but abundant life. A life where joy meets you each morning as you wake and an eager expectation of what the day will bring fills you down to your toes.

---

evening preceding All Saints Day, an observance on the Roman Catholic liturgical calendar to honor all those martyred for their faith in Christ. Established in 609 AD, it was originally held on May 12th/13th, but it was moved to October 31st/November 1st in the 8th century to oppose the pagan celebrations held at the time.

Life with Christ is an adventure. There are peaks and valleys, highs and lows, and sometimes disappointments, but it is a journey. It is a race we are running with the Creator of the Universe in the lead. (Hebrews 12:1-2) We are part of His story. We already know the end (if you don't know already, it's a good one), it's just all the bits in between that are a mystery to us.

When heaven and earth have passed away and we all sit down to watch how God's grand plan played out, we will be amazed at the impact we had and the role we played. All of the trials we went through, we will see the purpose and how God used them to build us up, to strengthen others, and to work through us to accomplish His plan[10]

God has a plan for you. He has invited you to enter in to be a part of His victory. Whatever fears you are facing today are just the enemy's attempts to squash you, to sit on you, and keep you down and out of the fun.

Decide right now he is not going to have his way, that in Christ, you are a conqueror.

Song of the Day

"Move" by Jesus Culture

On YouTube: https://www.youtube.com/watch?v=iOeb4j1hZeQ

---

[10] The topic of this building up through trials is the subject of my essay, "The Making of a Hero" in Volume 1, Issue 3 of An An Unexpected Journal. The issue as a whole is on "Courage, Strength, and Hope." You can read it online at http://anunexpectedjournal.com or find the book on Amazon.

Reflection

Do you see God as a loving Father who takes joy in you?

_____

_____

_____

_____

_____

How would you describe your relationship with God?

_____

_____

_____

_____

_____

Considering the thing that causes anxiety in your life, how does that illuminate the area in which you are not quite trusting God?

_____

_____

_____

_____

_____

If you have a fear about it, there is some part of God's nature that you do not fully understand or believe?

_____

_____

_____

_____

_____

Verses for the Day

1 John 4:18-19 NASB There is no fear in love, but perfect love casts out fear, because fear involves punishment, and the one who fears is not perfected in love. We love because He first loved us.

Romans 8:1-2 NASB Therefore there is now no condemnation for those who are in Christ Jesus. For the law of the Spirit of life in Christ Jesus has set you free from the law of sin and of death.

Romans 8:15-16 NASB For you have not received a spirit of slavery leading to fear again, but you have received a spirit of adoption as sons by which we cry out, "Abba! Father!" The Spirit Himself testifies with our spirit that we are children of God ."

Romans 8:37 KJV No, in all these things [trials and tribulations] we are more than conquerors through him who loved us.

Prayer

Father,

I thank you that you sent your son to free us from our fears and our wrongs. I thank you that your perfect love casts out fear. Help me to trust. Help my unbelief. Give me the gift of faith. Strengthen me with your spirit and help me clearly hear your voice and accomplish your will.

In Jesus's name. Amen.

OVERCOMING FEAR

We have spent seven days talking about and identifying fears. I hope this week-long devotional has helped to highlight hidden fears and root them out. The last day included a very key verse, 1 John 4:19 which reads "Perfect love casts out fear." Yes, it does mean the perfect love of Christ, but how does that perfect love become part of our lives? How does Christ's love for us help us with our own fears?

If you read the entire passage of chapter 4, it is a picture of what truly living in Christ is like. If he is love, and he shows love towards us, and we are in him, we must show love to others. That is how you get rid of fear . . . you must show love to others.

We all have friends to whom it is easy to show kindness. It is not enough, if there is any fear or anxiety in your life, it could be an indication that there is unforgiveness or hardness of heart somewhere.

I know forgiveness is a touchy thing and often people don't want to do it. So let me ask you this, do you want to continue to feel the way you are feeling or do you want to be free?

If the answer is the latter, let's go.

The Truth About Forgiveness

The most common misconception about forgiveness in our culture is that when you forgive someone, you just "forget" about the original offense. Sometimes people equate it with giving the wrong a pass. That is not it at all.

First, forgiveness is not a feeling, it is a choice. You choose to forgive and you do it out of obedience because we are told that our own sins will not be forgiven if we do not forgive others. (Matthew 18:21-22) When you pray and tell God that you choose to forgive the one who did the wrong, you release yourself from the emotional and spiritual tie between you and the other person that wrong has created. You are turning it over to God and leaving the next steps up to Him.

Second, forgiveness is not the same as restoration and it does not depend on the wrongdoer's repentance. Forgiveness is your choice. Repentance is up to the other person and it is entirely possible that they never repent.

Finally, forgiveness does not mean the relationship is restored. Particularly in abusive situations, it is not wise for the restoration to happen unless and until the wrongdoer has not only repented, but the sincerity of that repentance has been proven.

The picture of forgiveness is Jesus on the cross. While his accusers were in the middle of mocking him as he hung dying in agony, he said, "Forgive them, Father, for they don't even know what they are doing." He forgave us before we repented; however, we cannot be in relationship with him until we repent.

Repentance and Forgiveness: The Secret Weapons

Whatever the issue in your life, whether it is combating fears, health, family, or finances, the secret to victory in the situation involves one of two things: repentance or forgiveness. Sometimes both are required.

When you lose your peace and fear and confusion are operating in your life, ask the Holy Spirit if there is an area in your life where you need to confess and repent. If you ask and are sincere, he will tell you. He will bring a situation to mind and convict your heart. This may be an actual action, or it may be a mindset or heart attitude.

Don't be cavalier in the asking. Decide in advance that you are going to confess and be obedient, because if you ask him and then you refuse to repent of what he is showing you . . . you are then denying, quenching, the Holy Spirit. That is a dangerous place to be because it is the Holy Spirit who leads us into righteousness.

Also, ask if there is someone that you need to forgive. It is very easy to say, "I'm all good." But if the person comes to your mind, your heart clenches and you have this overwhelming desire to release a flow of verbal vomit, some forgiveness needs to happen there. Maybe there is a coldness, a hardness of heart when you think about them or the situation. That is hatred. Those feelings need to be confessed and repented of, forgive the person for whatever they did to offend you, and then ask God to bless them.

Is your back getting up just thinking about forgiving them? That is a definite sign it is needed.

Yes, I know, it is simple but it is not easy. It is hard. It is a decision you have to make. Do you want to be in relationship with God and have that love, joy, and peace that He promises, or do you want to stay where you are? How badly do you want to be free?

Layers of Forgiveness

This is another thing I have learned about forgiveness: there are layers. God will not ask you to deal with more than you can handle, and this also includes forgiveness. It may be that the circumstances are so painful and so raw that you can only handle a surface level of forgiveness. It may seem like the act of forgiving is a big thing for you at the time, but in reality, there are more issues lying underneath the surface.

If that is the case, the Holy Spirit will bring the person and the situation back around to go through another layer of forgiveness. If they come to your mind or a reference to that past time pops up, and you feel that tension that you thought you dealt with a long time ago, forgive them again. Again, God only asks of you what you can handle, you have come further now and can handle a deeper cleansing. Just remember that you have to continue to respond in obedience and forgive.

We are never done. Our sanctification process will continue until we see Jesus face to face, but it does get easier. As we practice obedience and forgiveness, the next time it comes up, it is easier to release.

NEXT STEPS

What's Next

Say you have done all that and there truly is no one or no attitude that is throwing up a barrier between you and God. You've confessed, you've forgiven and you've blessed, but still there is anxiety. If that is the case, you may be in a season of testing and training, a time to grow in your relationship with God. It is a time to learn to have a greater trust in God and to build your faith.

Even though forgiveness is hard and requires a humbling and submission of ourselves to God, it is easier and more clear-cut. We know what the issue is and what we have to do. The times of testing are harder. Like Job, we don't understand why certain things are happening or what specifically we have to do. It is in those times that we have to continue to testify to the goodness of God. As John wrote in his Revelation, we overcome by the "blood of the Lamb and the by the word of [our] testimony." (Rev 12:11)

This "testimony" is our agreement with God. We testify and come into agreement with God's Word about the matter.

After the Victory

You have identified this enemy spirit of fear, determined its tactics, designed and executed a plan of attack, and with the grace of God and the power of the Holy Spirit, you have overcome that particular fear. Write a short testimony, both as a reminder to yourself as well as something you can share with others.

Congratulate yourself on your successful campaign and battle won.

Guess what? The enemy will regroup, reassess, and come at you again. That is what he does and what he will continue to do until Jesus comes again and throws death and the grave into the abyss. This is where your testimony becomes helpful. It is not only to give glory to God as you share it with others, but it is a reminder for yourself when the enemy comes at you again.

If you are on the side of Christ, you will experience opposition. There will be trials. But Christ has already won the victory, and if we are obedient to him, every enemy attack only makes us stronger in Christ. That is why we are to "count it all joy" when troubles come because it is an opportunity for God to build our endurance and strengthen us.[11]

As someone once told me when I was discouraged when a situation did not turn out as, and when, I expected it . . . "The story isn't over yet."

---

[11] James 1:2-4 NLT "2 Dear brothers and sisters, when troubles of any kind come your way, consider it an opportunity for great joy. 3 For you know that when your faith is tested, your endurance has a chance to grow. 4 So let it grow, for when your endurance is fully developed, you will be perfect and complete, needing nothing."

THANK YOU

Thank you for reading #*NoFear*. If this book has had value to you and you have a testimony to share, I would love to hear about it. Please send thoughts or comments to feedback@raisedtowalk.org.

Reviews on Amazon are also much appreciated.

About the Author

Carla Alvarez is a mother to three, owner of Legacy Marketing Services, and a graduate of Houston Baptist University's Masters in Apologetics program. Her philosophy in both business and apologetics is if what we think affects what we do, then the "how" is just as important as the "what." As actions have a lasting impact, it is of utmost importance to develop right thoughts. She creates effective communications for clients at Legacy Marketing (www.legacymarketingservices.com) and writes about the Christian faith at RaisedtoWalk.org.

CONNECT

Want to go deeper in your walk with God? Sign up for my free newsletter at RaisedtoWalk.org and receive a free guide, "5 Tips to Connect with God in Scripture."

Social Media Connections

On Facebook:

https://facebook.com/RaisedtoWalk

On Instagram:

https://www.instagram.com/raisedtowalk/

On Twitter:

https://twitter.com/raisedtowalk

On Pinterest:

https://in.pinterest.com/raisedtowalk/

On Youtube:

https://www.youtube.com/user/RaisedtoWalkTV

More Works by C.M. Alvarez

An Unexpected Devotional

An Unexpected Devotional Workbook and Study Guide

Collaborative Works

An Unexpected Journal: The Abolition of Man, Vol 1, Issue 1 (Spring 2018)
"From the Green Book to The River: Lewis, Relativism, and Constructivism in Education"

An Unexpected Journal: Courage, Strength, & Hope, Vol 1, Issue 3 (Fall 2018).
"Hope, Life, and the Fountain of Trevi,"
"Lava: A Story of Love and Hope."
"The Making of a Hero."

An Unexpected Journal: Imagination, Vol 2, Issue 1 (Spring 2019).
"Imagination and Its Role in Faith."

An Unexpected Journal: Film & Music, Vol 2, Issue 3 (Summer 2019).
"Serenity and the Theodicy of Joss Whedon."

COMING FEBRUARY 2020

Straight Pathways

Money. Influence. Success. We chase these things thinking they will fulfill us, give us purpose. However, true fulfillment and peace come from knowing God and walking in His will.

See familiar stories from the Bible in a whole new way in *Straight Pathways*. C.M. Alvarez explores the ways both Bible heroes and anti-heroes can give us guidance in fulfilling our God-given destiny.

http://raisedtowalk.org/a/straight-pathways

My Testimony

When reading a book on faith, it's important to know where the author's faith lies. Why should you listen to the person when the book is just a front and doesn't line up with their life? This is my testimony about how I came to faith and who Jesus is to me.

Some people become a Christian because they are afraid of hell or because they want to be free of guilt, they want peace. But it wasn't like that for me. I grew up in a Christian home and both of my parents are believers. Especially in the life of my mom, I saw what having a relationship with God looked like. When she and my grandma would pray, the earth would move. Things changed. God answered their prayers.

I saw it was real and that is what I wanted. When I was seven, I prayed, acknowledged I was a sinner, and asked Jesus into my heart.

I was a Christian. I believed in Jesus as my Savior and knew I would go to heaven when I died, but I didn't feel like I had the same thing my mom did. I would pray, but if it was about something *really* important, I would ask my mom to pray for me. It just seemed like her prayers worked better.

Then I went through a divorce. It wasn't just a stressful and emotionally dark time, there was a literal darkness. But even in the midst of it all, I felt the actual presence of God. He was so present during that time that the fact that He was there was more true than the presence of the people I encountered day-to-day.

It didn't have anything to do with where I was spiritually at the time. It was as Psalm 34:18 says, "God draws near to the broken hearted. He rescues those whose spirits are crushed." That is where I was and He was there because I needed Him.

That was the change for me. I knew that I had the same relationship with God that my mom did. I knew God heard my prayers. Thinking otherwise was all in my head, it was not His heart towards me. I had to go through a very dark valley in order to realize that.

God is always drawing us into a deeper communion with Him. After the dark time passed, it was as if God set me down and said, "Okay, you can walk now." He met me where I was when I was too emotionally broken to do anything else, but once I began to heal, it was time to walk. I had to learn how to draw nearer to Him.

There were many things I had to learn, much bitterness I had to let go, and how to practice walking out the life of faith day-to-day. I had been in church my whole life, but salvation is much more than believing a set of doctrines. It is about going through this life with the Creator of the Universe as your guide. I had to learn how not only how to expect those answered prayers, but to expect His voice and to recognize that going to Him for guidance is a daily process.

This is not to say I have "arrived." You can learn a truth intellectually, but living out that truth is another thing entirely. There have been so many times when I come to a life situation that knocks me off balance, and then I'll go back and read something I wrote and think, "Yes, I know this." Knowing is the easy thing, it is the doing that is hard.

But it is in the doing that we meet the Presence of God. It is when we do what we already know that God brings us into a deeper fellowship with Him. It is as Reepicheep tells the new arrivals to Aslan's country in C.S. Lewis' *The Last Battle*, we are to "come further up, come further in."

Or do you not know that as many of us as were baptized into Christ Jesus were baptized into His death? 4 Therefore we were buried with Him through baptism into death, that just as Christ was raised from the dead by the glory of the Father, even so we also should walk in newness of life. Romans 6:3-4 NKJV

Therefore, since we are surrounded by such a huge crowd of witnesses to the life of faith, let us strip off every weight that slows us down, especially the sin that so easily trips us up. And let us run with endurance the race God has set before us. 2 We do this by keeping our eyes on Jesus, the champion who initiates and perfects our faith. Hebrews 12:1-2

THE FINAL DESTINATION

Thank you for reading #*NoFear: A 7-Day Devotional and Journal.* I hope that you have enjoyed the daily reflections, but more than that I hope that the words have helped you see Jesus, the Logos, Truth, and the Way, more clearly. As a pastor-apologist friend once stated, "all of these are just signposts, and you don't start on a journey to end up at a signpost. The final destination is Jesus.[12]"

If you have not yet set your course for Jesus as your final destination, don't stop with this devotional . . . which is simply a signpost. Enter the narrow door[13] and continue on your journey with Jesus.[14]

God loves you.[15] You were created in His image and he plannedh purpose for you before the world began.[16]

However, because God is holy and perfect, He cannot be in fellowship and communion the unholy and imperfect. Because our own wrong choices, thoughts, and

---

[12] Ryan Grube, "Apologetics Panel" (Panel discussion, HBU Apologetics Day, Woodlands Church, The Woodlands, TX. March 24, 2018.)"

[13] John 14:5-6 NASB "5 Thomas *said to Him, "Lord, we do not know where You are going, how do we know the way?" 6 Jesus *said to him, "I am the way, and the truth, and the life; no one comes to the Father but through Me."

[14] Matthew 7:13-14 NASB "13 "'Enter through the narrow gate; for the gate is wide and the way is broad that leads to destruction, and there are many who enter through it. 14 For the gate is small and the way is narrow that leads to life, and there are few who find it."

[15] John 3:16 KJV "For God so loved the world, that he gave his only begotten Son, that whosoever believeth in him should not perish, but have everlasting life."

[16] Ephesians 1:4-5 NLT "Even before he made the world, God loved us and chose us in Christ to be holy and without fault in his eyes. God decided in advance to adopt us into his own family by bringing us to himself through Jesus Christ. This is what he wanted to do, and it gave him great pleasure."

actions, that is what we have made ourselves to be . . . unholy and imperfect.

The all-encompassing word the Bible uses to describe that is translated in English as "sin." This is an old English archery term which means to "miss the mark." In God's eyes, the sort-of-okay things, the ones that aren't really bad but also aren't quite right, create just as much of a separation between us and Him as the big things we think of when we think of sin like adultery and murder.

God's Law is like a balloon. If the balloon is popped at any point, the whole thing is broken. In the same way, if we do wrong in one area, we are guilty of the whole.[17]

This leaves us in a predicament. We were made to commune with God, but we cannot because we are a mess. We are in a deep ravine that we cannot climb out of on our own. The more we try to work our way out, the bigger the hole we dig.[18]

We need someone to rescue us from the pit of our own creation.[19]

This is what Jesus did for us.

As noted apologist Lee Strobel has pointed out, the dilemma and the solution are given in one verse, Romans 6:23.[20]

> For the wages of sin is death, but the free gift of God is eternal life in Christ Jesus our Lord. Romans 6:23

Wages are something you earn for something you have done. Because we all have done things that go against God's universal moral law, we have earned death,

---

[17] James 2:10 NASB "For whoever keeps the whole law and yet stumbles in one point, he has become guilty of all."

[18] Isaiah 64:6 NASB. "For all of us have become like one who is unclean, And all our righteous deeds are like a filthy garment; And all of us wither like a leaf, And our iniquities, like the wind, take us away."

[19] Isaiah 63:16 NASB "For You are our Father, though Abraham does not know us And Israel does not recognize us You, O LORD, are our Father, Our Redeemer from of old is Your name."

[20] Lee Strobel, "Evangelism Methods" (class lecture, Evangelism, Houston Baptist University, Houston, TX. February 18, 2017.)

separation from God in eternity and spiritual separation from Him today.

But because God loves us, He made a way to reconcile us to Himself through Jesus. Jesus paid the price for our sins and satisfied the justice of the Law.

That penalty for what each of us has done has to be satisfied. The debt must be paid.

The Great Exchange

Because he was without sin, Jesus fulfilled the requirements of the Law himself. He took on our penalty and stood as the only righteous person in God's sight who had standing to atone for us, to make us right.[21]

He had not earned death, so death could not hold him.[22]

When Jesus, the Lamb of God, died on the cross, his blood atoned for (made right) our wrongs. This is the gift he is offering. His blood has already paid the price, but you must choose to receive it.[23]

---

[21] 2 Corinthians 5:21 NASB "He made Him who knew no sin to be sin on our behalf, so that we might become the righteousness of God in Him."

[22] 1 Corinthians 15:3-8 NLT "3 I passed on to you what was most important and what had also been passed on to me. Christ died for our sins, just as the Scriptures said. 4 He was buried, and he was raised from the dead on the third day, just as the Scriptures said. 5 He was seen by Peter[c] and then by the Twelve. 6 After that, he was seen by more than 500 of his followers at one time, most of whom are still alive, though some have died. 7 Then he was seen by James and later by all the apostles. 8 Last of all, as though I had been born at the wrong time, I also saw him."

Luke 13:23-25 NLT 23 Someone asked him, "Lord, will only a few be saved?" And He said to them, 24 "Strive to enter through the narrow door; for many, I tell you, will seek to enter and will not be able. 25 Once the head of the house gets up and shuts the door, and you begin to stand outside and knock on the door, saying, 'Lord, open up to us!' then He will answer and say to you, 'I do not know where you are from.'

[23] Romans 10:9 " . . . if you confess with your mouth Jesus as Lord, and believe in your heart that God raised Him from the dead, you will be saved;"

How to Find God

Admit that you have done wrong and need a Savior

Believe in Jesus as the sole source of your salvation.

Confess Jesus as your Lord, make him the Captain of your ship on life's journey.

> " . . . if you confess with your mouth Jesus as Lord, and believe in your heart that God raised Him from the dead, you will be saved;" - Romans 10:9

A New Creation

This is the Good News, that through the cross, our spirit that was dead in sin is born again. We have been made new, right in God's sight, and have the Holy Spirit within us.

> "Therefore if anyone is in Christ, he is a new creature; the old things passed away; behold, new things have come."
> 2 Corinthians 5:17

> "I have wiped out your transgressions like a thick cloud
> And your sins like a heavy mist. Return to Me, for I have redeemed you.
> Isaiah 44:22

PROGRESS JOURNAL

CONTINUING THE JOURNEY: A PROGRESS JOURNAL

We have spent the past week examining our fears and sources of anxiety, but change does not come by only knowing a thing, we must practice it. Following are journal pages for a month of reflection.

Take notes on when you woke up, your mental, physical and emotional states at the beginning of the day as well as the end. Choose a verse for the day. Now you may want to have a different verse for each day, or it might be a single verse to focus on over a period of time.

Record what you ate, if and when you had a devotional time and an exercise time, and particularly the sorts of things you are taking in. What types of things are you watching, reading, and listening to? What is the message of the TV shows or YouTube videos you are watching? What are the lyrics of the songs you are listening to? What are you reading? This includes social media.

Much attention is paid to the food we consume, but not as much is paid to the ideas and words we take in. As Paul writes in 2 Corinthians 10:15, "We demolish arguments and every pretension that sets itself up against the knowledge of God, and we take captive every thought to make it obedient to Christ." Most of us have enough trouble on our own keeping those negative thoughts out of our minds without external negative input. If we are taking in a steady diet of negativity and condemnation, why should we be surprised if our own thoughts are negative as well?

At the end of each day, pray and thank God for being with you and for all He has given you. Thank Him for being the God who heals and restores, the one who brings joy. Ask the Holy Spirit to illuminate your understanding and to show you the day's events from His perspective. Then write a reflection of the day. What was the highlight of the day? Thank God for his goodness and blessings. What was the low point of the day? Thank God for being with you through the time and thank Him or the work that

He is completing in you.

As you work through the journal, make a note of all of the things that are a part of your life and your mental emotional well-being. Do you see a connection between certain activities, certain people, or certain foods that correspond to low days?

At the end of a week, review your notes. Again, after asking the Holy Spirit to illuminate your understanding, write a reflection on the past week. What have you learned? What would you like to put into practice in the upcoming days? Continue for the rest of the month with times of reflection at the end of each week. At the end of the month, reflect on your progress. Can you see a change in your outlook? Do you see God in a different way?

8 Finally, brothers and sisters, whatever is true, whatever is noble, whatever is right, whatever is pure, whatever is lovely, whatever is admirable—if anything is excellent or praiseworthy—think about such things. 9 Whatever you have learned or received or heard from me, or seen in me—put it into practice. And the God of peace will be with you. – Philippians 4:8-9 NIV

I pray that the eyes of your heart may be enlightened in order that you may know the hope to which he has called you, the riches of his glorious inheritance in his holy people, and his incomparably great power for us who believe. – Ephesians 1:18-19 NIV

Date:

WAKEUP TIME

_____

MORNING MENTAL STATE

_____

_____

MENTAL INTAKE

WHAT I LISTENED TO:

_____

_____

WHAT I READ:

_____

_____

WHAT I WATCHED:

_____

_____

WHO I WAS AROUND:

_____

_____

_____

_____

DAILY INTAKE

BREAKFAST:

_____

_____

_____

LUNCH:

_____

_____

_____

DINNER:

_____

_____

_____

SNACKS:

_____

_____

_____

_____

_____

	Morning	Evening
MENTAL STATE		
PHYSICAL STATE		
SPIRITUAL STATE		

WHAT IS THE MAIN THING THAT STANDS OUT AS A FOCUS FOR THE DAY?

_____

_____

_____

WHAT WERE THE HIGH AND LOW POINTS OF THE DAY?

_____

_____

_____

REFLECTION FOR THE DAY:

_____

_____

_____

_____

_____

_____

Date:

WAKEUP TIME

_____

MORNING MENTAL STATE

_____

_____

MENTAL INTAKE

WHAT I LISTENED TO:

_____

_____

WHAT I READ:

_____

_____

WHAT I WATCHED:

_____

_____

WHO I WAS AROUND:

_____

_____

_____

DAILY INTAKE

BREAKFAST:

_____

_____

LUNCH:

_____

_____

DINNER:

_____

_____

SNACKS:

_____

_____

_____

_____

	Morning	Evening
Mental State		
Physical State		
Spiritual State		

What is the main thing that stands out as a focus for the day?

_____

_____

_____

What were the high and low points of the day?

_____

_____

_____

Reflection for the day:

_____

_____

_____

_____

_____

_____

Date:

WAKEUP TIME

_____

MORNING MENTAL STATE

_____

_____

MENTAL INTAKE

WHAT I LISTENED TO:

_____

_____

WHAT I READ:

_____

_____

WHAT I WATCHED:

_____

_____

WHO I WAS AROUND:

_____

_____

_____

DAILY INTAKE

BREAKFAST:

_____

_____

LUNCH:

_____

_____

DINNER:

_____

_____

SNACKS:

_____

_____

_____

_____

	Morning	Evening
MENTAL STATE		
PHYSICAL STATE		
SPIRITUAL STATE		

WHAT IS THE MAIN THING THAT STANDS OUT AS A FOCUS FOR THE DAY?

_____

_____

_____

WHAT WERE THE HIGH AND LOW POINTS OF THE DAY?

_____

_____

_____

REFLECTION FOR THE DAY:

_____

_____

_____

_____

_____

_____

Date:

Wakeup Time

_____

Morning Mental State

_____

_____

Mental Intake

What I Listened To:

_____

_____

What I Read:

_____

_____

What I Watched:

_____

_____

Who I Was Around:

_____

_____

_____

DAILY INTAKE

Breakfast:

_____

_____

Lunch:

_____

_____

Dinner:

_____

_____

Snacks:

_____

_____

_____

_____

	Morning	Evening
MENTAL STATE		
PHYSICAL STATE		
SPIRITUAL STATE		

WHAT IS THE MAIN THING THAT STANDS OUT AS A FOCUS FOR THE DAY?

_____

_____

_____

WHAT WERE THE HIGH AND LOW POINTS OF THE DAY?

_____

_____

_____

REFLECTION FOR THE DAY:

_____

_____

_____

_____

_____

Date:

WAKEUP TIME

_____

MORNING MENTAL STATE

_____

_____

MENTAL INTAKE

WHAT I LISTENED TO:

_____

_____

WHAT I READ:

_____

WHAT I WATCHED:

_____

_____

WHO I WAS AROUND:

_____

_____

_____

DAILY INTAKE

BREAKFAST:

_____

_____

LUNCH:

_____

_____

DINNER:

_____

_____

SNACKS:

_____

_____

_____

_____

	Morning	Evening
MENTAL STATE		
PHYSICAL STATE		
SPIRITUAL STATE		

WHAT IS THE MAIN THING THAT STANDS OUT AS A FOCUS FOR THE DAY?

_____

_____

_____

WHAT WERE THE HIGH AND LOW POINTS OF THE DAY?

_____

_____

_____

REFLECTION FOR THE DAY:

_____

_____

_____

_____

_____

_____

Date:

WAKEUP TIME

_____

MORNING MENTAL STATE

_____

_____

MENTAL INTAKE

WHAT I LISTENED TO:

_____

_____

WHAT I READ:

_____

_____

WHAT I WATCHED:

_____

_____

WHO I WAS AROUND:

_____

_____

_____

_____

DAILY INTAKE

BREAKFAST:

_____

_____

LUNCH:

_____

_____

DINNER:

_____

_____

SNACKS:

_____

_____

_____

_____

	Morning	Evening
MENTAL STATE		
PHYSICAL STATE		
SPIRITUAL STATE		

WHAT IS THE MAIN THING THAT STANDS OUT AS A FOCUS FOR THE DAY?

_____

_____

_____

WHAT WERE THE HIGH AND LOW POINTS OF THE DAY?

_____

_____

_____

REFLECTION FOR THE DAY:

_____

_____

_____

_____

_____

_____

Date:

Wakeup Time

_____

Morning Mental State

_____

_____

Mental Intake

What I Listened To:

_____

_____

What I Read:

_____

_____

What I Watched:

_____

_____

Who I Was Around:

_____

_____

_____

DAILY INTAKE

Breakfast:

_____

_____

Lunch:

_____

_____

Dinner:

_____

_____

Snacks:

_____

_____

_____

_____

	Morning	Evening
MENTAL STATE		
PHYSICAL STATE		
SPIRITUAL STATE		

WHAT IS THE MAIN THING THAT STANDS OUT AS A FOCUS FOR THE DAY?

_____

_____

_____

WHAT WERE THE HIGH AND LOW POINTS OF THE DAY?

_____

_____

_____

REFLECTION FOR THE DAY:

_____

_____

_____

_____

_____

_____

Date:

Wakeup Time

_____

Morning Mental State

_____

_____

Mental Intake

What I Listened To:

_____

_____

What I Read:

_____

_____

What I Watched:

_____

_____

Who I Was Around:

_____

_____

_____

DAILY INTAKE

Breakfast:

_____

_____

Lunch:

_____

_____

Dinner:

_____

_____

Snacks:

_____

_____

_____

_____

	Morning	**Evening**
MENTAL STATE		
PHYSICAL STATE		
SPIRITUAL STATE		

WHAT IS THE MAIN THING THAT STANDS OUT AS A FOCUS FOR THE DAY?

_____

_____

_____

WHAT WERE THE HIGH AND LOW POINTS OF THE DAY?

_____

_____

_____

REFLECTION FOR THE DAY:

_____

_____

_____

_____

_____

_____

Date:

WAKEUP TIME

_____

MORNING MENTAL STATE

_____

_____

MENTAL INTAKE

WHAT I LISTENED TO:

_____

_____

WHAT I READ:

_____

_____

WHAT I WATCHED:

_____

_____

WHO I WAS AROUND:

_____

_____

_____

DAILY INTAKE

BREAKFAST:

_____

_____

_____

LUNCH:

_____

_____

_____

DINNER:

_____

_____

_____

SNACKS:

_____

_____

_____

_____

_____

	Morning	Evening
MENTAL STATE		
PHYSICAL STATE		
SPIRITUAL STATE		

WHAT IS THE MAIN THING THAT STANDS OUT AS A FOCUS FOR THE DAY?

_____

_____

_____

WHAT WERE THE HIGH AND LOW POINTS OF THE DAY?

_____

_____

_____

REFLECTION FOR THE DAY:

_____

_____

_____

_____

_____

_____

Date:

WAKEUP TIME

_____

MORNING MENTAL STATE

_____

_____

MENTAL INTAKE

WHAT I LISTENED TO:

_____

_____

WHAT I READ:

_____

_____

WHAT I WATCHED:

_____

_____

WHO I WAS AROUND:

_____

_____

_____

_____

DAILY INTAKE

BREAKFAST:

_____

_____

_____

LUNCH:

_____

_____

_____

DINNER:

_____

_____

_____

SNACKS:

_____

_____

_____

_____

_____

	Morning	Evening
MENTAL STATE		
PHYSICAL STATE		
SPIRITUAL STATE		

WHAT IS THE MAIN THING THAT STANDS OUT AS A FOCUS FOR THE DAY?

_____

_____

_____

WHAT WERE THE HIGH AND LOW POINTS OF THE DAY?

_____

_____

_____

REFLECTION FOR THE DAY:

_____

_____

_____

_____

_____

_____

Date:

WAKEUP TIME

_____

MORNING MENTAL STATE

_____

_____

MENTAL INTAKE

WHAT I LISTENED TO:

_____

_____

WHAT I READ:

_____

_____

WHAT I WATCHED:

_____

_____

WHO I WAS AROUND:

_____

_____

_____

DAILY INTAKE

BREAKFAST:

_____

_____

_____

LUNCH:

_____

_____

_____

DINNER:

_____

_____

_____

SNACKS:

_____

_____

_____

_____

_____

	Morning	Evening
MENTAL STATE		
PHYSICAL STATE		
SPIRITUAL STATE		

WHAT IS THE MAIN THING THAT STANDS OUT AS A FOCUS FOR THE DAY?

_____

_____

_____

WHAT WERE THE HIGH AND LOW POINTS OF THE DAY?

_____

_____

_____

REFLECTION FOR THE DAY:

_____

_____

_____

_____

_____

_____

Date:

Wakeup Time

_____

Morning Mental State

_____

_____

Mental Intake

What I Listened To:

_____

_____

What I Read:

_____

_____

What I Watched:

_____

_____

Who I Was Around:

_____

_____

_____

_____

DAILY INTAKE

Breakfast:

_____

_____

Lunch:

_____

_____

Dinner:

_____

_____

Snacks:

_____

_____

_____

_____

_____

	Morning	Evening
MENTAL STATE		
PHYSICAL STATE		
SPIRITUAL STATE		

WHAT IS THE MAIN THING THAT STANDS OUT AS A FOCUS FOR THE DAY?

_____

_____

_____

WHAT WERE THE HIGH AND LOW POINTS OF THE DAY?

_____

_____

_____

REFLECTION FOR THE DAY:

_____

_____

_____

_____

_____

_____

Date:

WAKEUP TIME

_____

MORNING MENTAL STATE

_____

_____

MENTAL INTAKE

WHAT I LISTENED TO:

_____

_____

WHAT I READ:

_____

_____

WHAT I WATCHED:

_____

_____

WHO I WAS AROUND:

_____

_____

_____

_____

DAILY INTAKE

BREAKFAST:

_____

_____

LUNCH:

_____

_____

DINNER:

_____

_____

SNACKS:

_____

_____

_____

_____

	Morning	Evening
MENTAL STATE		
PHYSICAL STATE		
SPIRITUAL STATE		

WHAT IS THE MAIN THING THAT STANDS OUT AS A FOCUS FOR THE DAY?

_____

_____

_____

WHAT WERE THE HIGH AND LOW POINTS OF THE DAY?

_____

_____

_____

REFLECTION FOR THE DAY:

_____

_____

_____

_____

_____

_____

Date:

Wakeup Time
_____

Morning Mental State
_____
_____

Mental Intake

What I Listened To:
_____
_____

What I Read:
_____
_____

What I Watched:
_____
_____

Who I Was Around:
_____
_____
_____
_____

DAILY INTAKE

Breakfast:
_____
_____
_____

Lunch:
_____
_____
_____

Dinner:
_____
_____
_____

Snacks:
_____
_____
_____
_____

	Morning	**Evening**
MENTAL STATE		
PHYSICAL STATE		
SPIRITUAL STATE		

WHAT IS THE MAIN THING THAT STANDS OUT AS A FOCUS FOR THE DAY?

_____

_____

_____

WHAT WERE THE HIGH AND LOW POINTS OF THE DAY?

_____

_____

_____

REFLECTION FOR THE DAY:

_____

_____

_____

_____

_____

_____

Date:

WAKEUP TIME

_____

MORNING MENTAL STATE

_____

_____

MENTAL INTAKE

WHAT I LISTENED TO:

_____

_____

WHAT I READ:

_____

_____

WHAT I WATCHED:

_____

_____

WHO I WAS AROUND:

_____

_____

_____

_____

DAILY INTAKE

BREAKFAST:

_____

_____

_____

LUNCH:

_____

_____

_____

DINNER:

_____

_____

_____

SNACKS:

_____

_____

_____

_____

_____

	Morning	Evening
MENTAL STATE		
PHYSICAL STATE		
SPIRITUAL STATE		

WHAT IS THE MAIN THING THAT STANDS OUT AS A FOCUS FOR THE DAY?

_____

_____

_____

WHAT WERE THE HIGH AND LOW POINTS OF THE DAY?

_____

_____

_____

REFLECTION FOR THE DAY:

_____

_____

_____

_____

_____

_____

Date:

Wakeup Time

_____

Morning Mental State

_____

_____

Mental Intake

What I Listened To:

_____

_____

What I Read:

_____

_____

What I Watched:

_____

_____

Who I Was Around:

_____

_____

_____

DAILY INTAKE

Breakfast:

_____

_____

_____

Lunch:

_____

_____

_____

Dinner:

_____

_____

_____

Snacks:

_____

_____

_____

_____

_____

	Morning	Evening
MENTAL STATE		
PHYSICAL STATE		
SPIRITUAL STATE		

WHAT IS THE MAIN THING THAT STANDS OUT AS A FOCUS FOR THE DAY?

_____

_____

_____

WHAT WERE THE HIGH AND LOW POINTS OF THE DAY?

_____

_____

_____

REFLECTION FOR THE DAY:

_____

_____

_____

_____

_____

_____

Date:

Wakeup Time

_____

Morning Mental State

_____

_____

Mental Intake

What I Listened To:

_____

_____

What I Read:

_____

_____

What I Watched:

_____

_____

Who I Was Around:

_____

_____

_____

DAILY INTAKE

Breakfast:

_____

_____

_____

Lunch:

_____

_____

_____

Dinner:

_____

_____

_____

Snacks:

_____

_____

_____

_____

	Morning	Evening
MENTAL STATE		
PHYSICAL STATE		
SPIRITUAL STATE		

WHAT IS THE MAIN THING THAT STANDS OUT AS A FOCUS FOR THE DAY?

_____

_____

_____

WHAT WERE THE HIGH AND LOW POINTS OF THE DAY?

_____

_____

_____

REFLECTION FOR THE DAY:

_____

_____

_____

_____

_____

_____

Date:

WAKEUP TIME

_____

MORNING MENTAL STATE

_____

_____

MENTAL INTAKE

WHAT I LISTENED TO:

_____

_____

WHAT I READ:

_____

_____

WHAT I WATCHED:

_____

_____

WHO I WAS AROUND:

_____

_____

_____

DAILY INTAKE

BREAKFAST:

_____

_____

LUNCH:

_____

_____

DINNER:

_____

_____

SNACKS:

_____

_____

_____

_____

	Morning	**Evening**
MENTAL STATE		
PHYSICAL STATE		
SPIRITUAL STATE		

WHAT IS THE MAIN THING THAT STANDS OUT AS A FOCUS FOR THE DAY?

_____

_____

_____

WHAT WERE THE HIGH AND LOW POINTS OF THE DAY?

_____

_____

_____

REFLECTION FOR THE DAY:

_____

_____

_____

_____

_____

Date:

WAKEUP TIME

_____

MORNING MENTAL STATE

_____

_____

MENTAL INTAKE

WHAT I LISTENED TO:

_____

_____

WHAT I READ:

_____

_____

WHAT I WATCHED:

_____

_____

WHO I WAS AROUND:

_____

_____

_____

DAILY INTAKE

BREAKFAST:

_____

_____

_____

LUNCH:

_____

_____

_____

DINNER:

_____

_____

_____

SNACKS:

_____

_____

_____

_____

_____

	Morning	Evening
MENTAL STATE		
PHYSICAL STATE		
SPIRITUAL STATE		

WHAT IS THE MAIN THING THAT STANDS OUT AS A FOCUS FOR THE DAY?

_____

_____

_____

WHAT WERE THE HIGH AND LOW POINTS OF THE DAY?

_____

_____

_____

REFLECTION FOR THE DAY:

_____

_____

_____

_____

_____

_____

Date:

WAKEUP TIME

_____

MORNING MENTAL STATE

_____

_____

MENTAL INTAKE

WHAT I LISTENED TO:

_____

_____

WHAT I READ:

_____

_____

WHAT I WATCHED:

_____

_____

WHO I WAS AROUND:

_____

_____

_____

_____

DAILY INTAKE

BREAKFAST:

_____

_____

LUNCH:

_____

_____

DINNER:

_____

_____

SNACKS:

_____

_____

_____

_____

	Morning	Evening
MENTAL STATE		
PHYSICAL STATE		
SPIRITUAL STATE		

WHAT IS THE MAIN THING THAT STANDS OUT AS A FOCUS FOR THE DAY?

_____

_____

_____

WHAT WERE THE HIGH AND LOW POINTS OF THE DAY?

_____

_____

_____

REFLECTION FOR THE DAY:

_____

_____

_____

_____

_____

_____

Date:

WAKEUP TIME

_____

MORNING MENTAL STATE

_____

_____

MENTAL INTAKE

WHAT I LISTENED TO:

_____

_____

WHAT I READ:

_____

_____

WHAT I WATCHED:

_____

_____

WHO I WAS AROUND:

_____

_____

_____

DAILY INTAKE

BREAKFAST:

_____

_____

_____

LUNCH:

_____

_____

_____

DINNER:

_____

_____

_____

SNACKS:

_____

_____

_____

_____

	Morning	Evening
MENTAL STATE		
PHYSICAL STATE		
SPIRITUAL STATE		

WHAT IS THE MAIN THING THAT STANDS OUT AS A FOCUS FOR THE DAY?

_____

_____

_____

WHAT WERE THE HIGH AND LOW POINTS OF THE DAY?

_____

_____

_____

REFLECTION FOR THE DAY:

_____

_____

_____

_____

_____

Date:

Wakeup Time

_____

Morning Mental State

_____

_____

Mental Intake

What I Listened To:

_____

_____

What I Read:

_____

_____

What I Watched:

_____

_____

Who I Was Around:

_____

_____

_____

DAILY INTAKE

Breakfast:

_____

_____

_____

Lunch:

_____

_____

_____

Dinner:

_____

_____

_____

Snacks:

_____

_____

_____

_____

	Morning	Evening
MENTAL STATE		
PHYSICAL STATE		
SPIRITUAL STATE		

WHAT IS THE MAIN THING THAT STANDS OUT AS A FOCUS FOR THE DAY?

_____

_____

_____

WHAT WERE THE HIGH AND LOW POINTS OF THE DAY?

_____

_____

_____

REFLECTION FOR THE DAY:

_____

_____

_____

_____

_____

_____

Date:

WAKEUP TIME

_____

MORNING MENTAL STATE

_____

_____

MENTAL INTAKE

WHAT I LISTENED TO:

_____

_____

WHAT I READ:

_____

_____

WHAT I WATCHED:

_____

_____

WHO I WAS AROUND:

_____

_____

_____

_____

DAILY INTAKE

BREAKFAST:

_____

_____

_____

LUNCH:

_____

_____

_____

DINNER:

_____

_____

_____

SNACKS:

_____

_____

_____

_____

_____

	Morning	Evening
MENTAL STATE		
PHYSICAL STATE		
SPIRITUAL STATE		

WHAT IS THE MAIN THING THAT STANDS OUT AS A FOCUS FOR THE DAY?

_____

_____

_____

WHAT WERE THE HIGH AND LOW POINTS OF THE DAY?

_____

_____

_____

REFLECTION FOR THE DAY:

_____

_____

_____

_____

_____

_____

Date:

WAKEUP TIME

_____

MORNING MENTAL STATE

_____

_____

MENTAL INTAKE

WHAT I LISTENED TO:

_____

_____

WHAT I READ:

_____

_____

WHAT I WATCHED:

_____

_____

WHO I WAS AROUND:

_____

_____

_____

_____

DAILY INTAKE

BREAKFAST:

_____

_____

LUNCH:

_____

_____

DINNER:

_____

_____

SNACKS:

_____

_____

_____

_____

	Morning	**Evening**
MENTAL STATE		
PHYSICAL STATE		
SPIRITUAL STATE		

WHAT IS THE MAIN THING THAT STANDS OUT AS A FOCUS FOR THE DAY?

_____

_____

_____

WHAT WERE THE HIGH AND LOW POINTS OF THE DAY?

_____

_____

_____

REFLECTION FOR THE DAY:

_____

_____

_____

_____

_____

Date:

Wakeup Time

_____

Morning Mental State

_____

_____

Mental Intake

What I Listened To:

_____

_____

What I Read:

_____

_____

What I Watched:

_____

_____

Who I Was Around:

_____

_____

_____

DAILY INTAKE

Breakfast:

_____

_____

_____

Lunch:

_____

_____

Dinner:

_____

_____

Snacks:

_____

_____

_____

_____

_____

	Morning	Evening
MENTAL STATE		
PHYSICAL STATE		
SPIRITUAL STATE		

WHAT IS THE MAIN THING THAT STANDS OUT AS A FOCUS FOR THE DAY?

_____

_____

_____

WHAT WERE THE HIGH AND LOW POINTS OF THE DAY?

_____

_____

_____

REFLECTION FOR THE DAY:

_____

_____

_____

_____

_____

_____

Date:

Wakeup Time

_____

Morning Mental State

_____

_____

Mental Intake

What I Listened To:

_____

_____

What I Read:

_____

_____

What I Watched:

_____

_____

Who I Was Around:

_____

_____

_____

_____

DAILY INTAKE

Breakfast:

_____

_____

_____

Lunch:

_____

_____

_____

Dinner:

_____

_____

_____

Snacks:

_____

_____

_____

_____

_____

	Morning	Evening
MENTAL STATE		
PHYSICAL STATE		
SPIRITUAL STATE		

WHAT IS THE MAIN THING THAT STANDS OUT AS A FOCUS FOR THE DAY?

_____

_____

_____

WHAT WERE THE HIGH AND LOW POINTS OF THE DAY?

_____

_____

_____

REFLECTION FOR THE DAY:

_____

_____

_____

_____

_____

_____

Date:

Wakeup Time

_____

Morning Mental State

_____

_____

Mental Intake

What I Listened To:

_____

_____

What I Read:

_____

_____

What I Watched:

_____

_____

Who I Was Around:

_____

_____

_____

DAILY INTAKE

Breakfast:

_____

_____

Lunch:

_____

_____

Dinner:

_____

_____

Snacks:

_____

_____

_____

_____

	Morning	Evening
MENTAL STATE		
PHYSICAL STATE		
SPIRITUAL STATE		

WHAT IS THE MAIN THING THAT STANDS OUT AS A FOCUS FOR THE DAY?

_____

_____

_____

WHAT WERE THE HIGH AND LOW POINTS OF THE DAY?

_____

_____

_____

REFLECTION FOR THE DAY:

_____

_____

_____

_____

_____

Date:

Wakeup Time

_____

Morning Mental State

_____

_____

Mental Intake

What I Listened To:

_____

_____

What I Read:

_____

_____

What I Watched:

_____

_____

Who I Was Around:

_____

_____

_____

DAILY INTAKE

Breakfast:

_____

_____

_____

Lunch:

_____

_____

Dinner:

_____

_____

_____

Snacks:

_____

_____

_____

_____

_____

	Morning	Evening
MENTAL STATE		
PHYSICAL STATE		
SPIRITUAL STATE		

WHAT IS THE MAIN THING THAT STANDS OUT AS A FOCUS FOR THE DAY?

_____

_____

_____

WHAT WERE THE HIGH AND LOW POINTS OF THE DAY?

_____

_____

_____

REFLECTION FOR THE DAY:

_____

_____

_____

_____

_____

Date:

Wakeup Time

_____

Morning Mental State

_____

_____

Mental Intake

What I Listened To:

_____

_____

What I Read:

_____

_____

What I Watched:

_____

_____

Who I Was Around:

_____

_____

_____

_____

DAILY INTAKE

Breakfast:

_____

_____

Lunch:

_____

_____

Dinner:

_____

_____

Snacks:

_____

_____

_____

_____

_____

	Morning	Evening
MENTAL STATE		
PHYSICAL STATE		
SPIRITUAL STATE		

WHAT IS THE MAIN THING THAT STANDS OUT AS A FOCUS FOR THE DAY?

_____

_____

_____

WHAT WERE THE HIGH AND LOW POINTS OF THE DAY?

_____

_____

_____

REFLECTION FOR THE DAY:

_____

_____

_____

_____

_____

_____

notes